QUARRY CROSS

Robin Behn

a plume editions book

AN IMPRINT OF MADHAT PRESS
ASHEVILLE, NORTH CAROLINA

MadHat Press
MadHat Incorporated
PO Box 8364, Asheville, NC 28814

The Library of Congress has assigned
this edition a Control Number of
2018930558

ISBN: 978-1-941196-64-9 (paperback)

Cover painting by Melissa Herrington
Author photo by Isabella Means
Cover design by Marc Vincenz

Plume Editions
an imprint of MadHat Press
www.MadHat-Press.com

First Printing

QUARRY CROSS

For Andy

Table of Contents

I

II

I

Shatter

Anyway, the shattering. It hardly matters
of what anymore. The deer have not appeared,
though *they* know with what they rhyme,
perfectly and not.
Instead, what I got, on the path,
spooked by my traveling shadow,
shattered now and then by spidery
branches shattering the sun,
was a rabbit, changeling of *speed* and *freeze.*
Once the poem's changed from *shatter's ae*s to *speed* and *freeze's ee*s
it is better to be in.
There is an improvement.
See? Be? Me? The sound
becomes a little thing to worship
that cordons us off from how the mind
goes harvesting shatter after shatter,
poor pattern-hungry mind.
Now there is a little thing to worship,
the way a metronome is said to aid some kinds of minds
with meting out the chaos.
So, anyway, we can sort things out now.
The deer and rabbit into the "brown fur" box,
and you and me, Reader, into the "flesh and probably clothed" box.
Or you and the deer into the delicate basket of
"the things we go on, on faith, about"
whilst me and my rabbit are unpacking our things again this
        summer
in the Sturdily Conjured Mammals' Cabin.
Anyway, the shattering. If you want an example there is
my (favorite, dead) uncle's teeth
against my (dead) mother's wildly bleeding forehead,

3

the baseball whistling past their scrambled mitts
on out into the Great Depression,
and the one about death-do-we-part, and the one about
the big rock that keeps on shattering all the air forever ever since
they found it had been rolled away.
We're drawn to certain kinds of shatterings
even if no one else is. Though company's
nice, as in, Come on over y'all for the next shattering,
here, have my beeper or are you already
on the transplant team…? The rabbit ran so far
(he was a pre-teen rabbit), so far ahead on the path,
that by the time all of his back-glancing statues (Orphie! No!)
had dumped back into his fluid self
—filmstrip rabbit back into movie rabbit—
he was an acre, at least, from his mom.
He found her again or he didn't,
the way when glass shatters it
always leaves behind a map of your hometown
and the house where you grew up
either swings there in the web or cuts you silently to shreds.
Forget about drinking and forget seeing anything clearly.
Anyway, the rabbit. Anyway, the day.
Though the deer, doe-and-fawn,
my "Deers Against All Shattering,"
have not quite yet appeared.

Here at the Scene

Deborah Digges, 1950–2009

How will I tell her particular tale
who now belongs to earth
where we are all the same

who had a heart-shaped face
and a lioness heart
the wild laugh of all the saints
drunk at once

who given a field of wildflowers
would wade blindly in
until their exquisite faces
turned her mind to lace

and when a rhythm came to her
in language or in love
would ride the horse of it
across the far pasture

and through the jagged woods till
it came away in strips
and she was in the clearing again
afloat on her own words
a little blissful while

Some of the rest's a strobe-light slideshow too
wild boring stupid hard giddy tender to tell

and the tiny totem witnesses hanging
in her kitchen in the rickety printer's drawer
—thimbles and thimble-sized porcelain dolls shards
from three continents itty-bitty Dutch shoes a legion

of wings rings changeling leafy rinds a matchstick
flute errant buttons requisite china horse the
rough-scissored locket-shaped faces of her
boys as boys—

do not quit their dusty little prison cells
to leap into a diorama that would explain

Here at the edge of the field
the sparrows alight on the silence
I have always kept
but they can only speak
untranslated Sparrow now

Here is what poetry comes to:
the stadium's tall equine stature the
far stables smearing the distance her
particular huge hoofprint breaking the planet's crust …

Genius, you tyrant,
no oats!

irishtune.info

Without wanting to get too involved in relationships to the rest of
    the body.
Without wanting to get too involved in a clear sign, I would venture.
This is, frankly, the great weakness.
On the other hand.
Contrary to the above rules a family theory, a tinker story.
Large scale structures susceptible to people who disagree.
She actively plays. I suggest. You might consider.
Well-known borderline cases, a very obvious error.
So you should just look.
I name you in the clear-cut case.
Older names over newer names.
Just my decision. Totally wrong!
I assign you. I have found you. The idea is to send you.
"Older is better."
I have also consistently held myself.
I enter the exact location.
It means that I have listened.
I have been verified, slightly more relaxed.
If you debate 65 million potential relationships
then I don't play. I may abandon use.
I changed something on November 12.
Please use the formula.
"Personally verified" means
I have listened, I have linked.
I'd be very happy if you could prove me wrong,
usually, seamlessly, finally, regardless.
What do you consider traditional?
Then what this allows is the sometimes marked differences.
I would venture more hands.

Very rare, clear-cut case:
a significant body.
This is, frankly, the great weakness of all.

The Cliffs of Moher

What if someone took such
a large bite out of you
your crying swelled out
to the end of the world?

How would you bear the onlookers
in their painfully blue and red jackets,
your picture taken and taken
from a distance judged safe?

As when they brought the boy in
from the wolves who raised him,
with a pike and a cage.
No one could talk to him.

Their persistence sounded
to him like crashing.
They made of him a living
monument and, a few of them, a living.

The doctors passed him off
till not even the lowliest expert
had a use.
What was there to do?

He who was neither
wolf nor man, who bit back
at their entreaties
with his chiseled face?

Here is a tune
to help him dance or sleep.
It is a little like
the music in him

which is to say a moth'ring
mouth and a maw.
A mordant, dormant tune
from which he cannot fall.

The Cliffs of Moher

Inventory at Dusk

for my father

One dark blue hospital gown
whose necklace of snaps shone
like a tiny constellation.

One vase of pussywillows
and another of long-stemmed swabs'
soft buds aswarm in contemplation.

Slumberous music, cello
(although he played piano). So,
one well-intended notion.

The small TV turned off
so there's a frame around the dark.
Plenteous devotions.

So at first I was not needed.
I knelt under the sky blue sky
of the lips, and traced the final motion

where the hand had curled
like a fern re-furled
to its first consecration.

What could I say to you, loose soul,
my confidant, new orphan,
shy of brash contrition?

The window stayed closed.
It wanted that, the soul.
Still stubborn about asking for directions.

I stroked its ether hair.
It stroked—the air.
And I sang. Not to my companion,

who is what singing is.
I sang to my father's not-knowing,
(the soul was already going)

I sang for his wild mouth.
I sang instead of truth.
I sang for a place to lean on.

And opened the window then.
A little. I did. But first I combed his hair
like going over the ocean.

The Star above the Garter

She is waiting for him outside the dance hall. In deepest snow. She has changed into her boots, the brown ones, the brown leather ones the color of a brown thrasher and a chestnut horse. Stamping there. Breathing in little swords and whips, the air snapping in half from the cold. Her big mittens on, the beefy fur-lined ones. And her dance shoes over her shoulder tied together by their long laces in a clumsy epaulet. She is waiting for orders, for something to happen, the way the dance caller made everyone swing and star, gypsy and progress, forward and back like bright gears in a mazy kaleidoscope that would be a perfect model of time itself were it not for the fact that the tune began and ended. It just ended. She's sweating beneath her wool coat, waiting for him outside the grange.

What was it she had almost told him when they circled their tight circle before passing on to the next? The breath reeling out of her, their gazes locked to keep from spinning off the edge of this particular earth to where the music comes from, somewhere so long ago and far away it cannot possibly be alive anymore, like light from a long-dead star—except that it is, it was, being played, still, by the fiddle and bow, the wooden door sawed in half again and again, portal to the underworld that seals and seals itself almost back up as the song spools out ...

It was his hand, the calm, dry, pulsing, uncomplicated balance of his hand, and then the essential distance up to his face, the simple beard and attentive lop of dark hair and the quick, almost canine, grin. How is it that on this particular evening everyone has been called up out of their sideline chairs, the dead crossing over to take hands with the living, to come, when you least expect them, down the line? Why did you come here tonight when you could have been doing the dishes, furiously polishing old harms? Why this tribal dance, this stylized joining of *he* and *she*, when you actually hunger for the private dance in living room, porch, kitchen, bed, before anyone has ever chosen to unsubscribe from earth, to purposefully drown?

She is standing in the snow. It feels deep enough to drown her. Waiting for him to leave by himself which is how, she thinks, the dead are likely to travel when they come back to poke the ashes of the earthly dance. Her body, sweat right through, taking on the chill.

Star, it's your music, but it is not your fault.

Someone, ask her back in for the last waltz.

The Star Above the Garter

The Stanzas Combine at Dusk, Across and Down

past the room where we meet this time
the rise and fall of pines
makes one jagged shape
the falling sun falls through

where a giant's left his saw out
blade side up working itself away
to finish off the bloody dusk
but here, close up, green needles

soft green needles in our mouths
terribly, terribly soft green needles
and the continuous gorgeousness
of trading them back and forth

the falling sun falling makes
his darkness rise and fall and pine
for the room
where we met before he died

the polishing of dusk
to blood's giant blood
is work, is what work is,
blame side up

blame the jagged past
continue terribly, terribly
green need in all my mouths
until closed, closed up

What you told me,

word on word like
straws in a fist, the short and the long of it,
the hollowed-out, already-tanned
midnight paste of it, some thing about
a boy, some thing about a knife nearby, a boy-voice
buckling up through tonnage of wet sand, a game, just
a game, the straw in the mouth of it,
filled with the collapse of it, the torpor and collide, some
thing about forgetting, the mouth-meat abandoned, but
speaking, speaking now, sharpening
the blame of it, shimmying the damp of it, a drifting
of the rack of bones the cloth-covered
face is, a sinking contingency, conscripted
awe of the boy *the boy who lived*, his room
the next room, straws in a fist, stick slapped across your
palm, his room in Athens now, his room on the moon,
his door in the mountain, skull and crossbones in the mountain
collapsing, time
spitting, the hours running down on him
who you are not the father of, not the
twin brother of, the long and the short of it,
the single responsible hour, some boss breathing
down on it, some place where the dead
line up for their silly food, the saying of the meat of it,
the things that must be seen to, the boy
not your boy, the straw in his mouth,
the thud and the glance as you
watch me for a sign, the boy
not your boy no of course no
t you rs, but the weight and the heat,

the grill and the grid the ghosts
still sift through, the fishy air jammed with them,
leaves in your mouth, the radical random
darkness still settling, the leaves, the tree,
the tree the boy shakes to death
the next day, rooted, but wounded, a
purple leafy darkness ashamed, the leaf-sounds undoably
overlapped, the grimble and soak, the
rot and the drift of throat of dark throat,
the suck and the quiet now, quiet, shhh, the
thrum of these particular these
boy-ridden glades.

In a Vodka Vein

"Work, car, drive, lot, park, bucks, bag, car, home, ether, sleep, work, repeat."

Item: why she left him

"Work, car, drive, lot, park, bucks, bag, car, home, evening-blood-bobbing-with-gondolas, sleep, work, repeat."

Language, I see you are trying to make yourself pretty.

"The little people in the blood in the gondolas sipping the beautiful water of life from their beautiful little matching glasses."

Item: liver's svelte waistline

Item: the shapes of pears

Language, how do you make the little glasses.

"Smelt things into liquid and blow it."

Item: giddy flocks of experts in the trees.

Language, what things do you smelt?

"Work, car, drive, lot, park, bucks, bag, car, home, tongue-tied-tongue-of-opaque-glass, sleep, work, repeat."

Item: the brown bag's neck twisted like her broomstick skirt.

Why.

"Everybody on the gondolas all wants a glass glass
so you have to keep on blowing it."

Blowing what.

"Work, car, drive, lot, park, bucks, bag, car, home, chance, sleep,
work, repeat."

Item: the life of the woman in the skirt, dancing upside down in the
bag.

What is it distilled from.

"Sea bellow."

Language let's fix your hair a little. There.

"*"

What are the rocks in the glass.

"War, lot, park, bucks, bag, car, home, one-of-a-kind-prehistoric-beasts-
suffocated-in-permafrost-melting-back-to-life, sleep, work, repeat."

No what are the little rocks in the little glasses in the little people's
hands in the little gondolas?

"Earth-murk that hardened into pellets of the human penchant for
oblivion."

No what are the rocks?

"Million-dollar crystals of the waters of Lethe."

No what are the rocks?

"That hardened like snowflakes around dust's signature?"

No What What What

"Depressun Concussun Fulcrum Possum"

"Evolushun, bad dog, we can't slobber you pup."

""Eggsellent, eggsellent.""

Thee and me, Love, camped below the freezing point.

Item: one long-stemmed glass rose

"And in the next tent Ivan the Terrible takes a well-earned beheading break to establish his vodka monopoly!"

As night creaks on, stepping over glass.

"Would you like that with poetry."

What flavor.

"Whacha got."

Acorn, horseradish, strychnine, mint, red pepper, death, ginger, chocolate.

"Naw. Did you know you can fill a musket with it."

You're getting warmer.

"They used to fill their muskrats with it."

Car, lot, drive, park, bucks, bag, home,   ,   ,   ,

*1. bedraggled wing   2. flammable fist-mitten

From the '60s

Here is the official entry. One among the many.
Here are the flip-tops and flip-flops
and the nails and the rock and the song, off-key.

Here is the offer. Here, a little holster.
A lipstick of discontinued hue.
All of these items are key.

We are not having awful dinner.
We are in the business of getting thinner.
Here is the throat's little key.

Here is supposed to and Kant.
The Elect Lillies platform and its chant.
And a key to the swivel of the skull-shaped chair.

Here shimmers love, the porch and the wind,
the quiet and the prodigal care.
Out of that fire, a key of twisted hair.

Here is What did you do to your hair?
Here is a shag and a brag and a dare.
Bobby-pin jaws are a key to a mouth
  wired shut by kisses and the rest.

We are not remembering who was remiss.
We are going forward like a pony through this,
blinders and fetlock-deep snow and the abyss.

Here is the smokescreen that was her eyes.
How is it possible she drove home?
Where is the key to unfasten the guise

she's worn ever after and a fetching disguise
of shredded shadow across her eyes.
—*The keening? Still? of wolves?* did you say?

We are using "and" in today's report because it doesn't cause a fuss
and stir up the sound still circling her face.
Now we'll file *that* and *that* and *that* back in their place.

I Never Promised You a Rose Garden

The prairie knows,
down below the downy
tops of its legions of thistles, down along the lengths of
its damp stalks, down through the
fire-toughened grizzle of root mat,
way down in the gracious underworld
of ant, bulb, carapace, loam,

and I know,
down below the beard of the teacher
who said how silly to write
as if we know what nature is "feeling," down below
the shelves of art constructed
from the previous century's top half of the brain
scooting on its gray mass without a nerve-root,

and I know from my own resistance
to the depth of this thing—

how I tried to eat through it, drive through it,
order it for lunch or to its execution,
how I've driven a wedge of amnesia between
that half of my life and this—

but now it's back, hovering in the dream—the ratty, mold-
bedazzled, urine-colored pages and her glasses,
shiny stop signs and the face behind the glasses, the
nameless, squinting firmament of flesh

how I was that girl
who read that book

and felt myself carried away
to the padded room there being
nothing else to lean on, nothing
to gather round me like a quilted coat
or a coat of arms or a leopard-collared coat
or any arms at all
                                   and felt
myself above myself, a switch
flipped, the docking unlocked:

At least between the book and me
there were two who on earth …

I wasn't the only, the craziest one …

as if when they handed out souls, mine
had come without the body,
and no one had told the body
till the others, shining, *saw,*
and ran …

I carry her with me, the girl with the paperback
tucked under her sweaty arm,
and I carry the room she read it in,
pink as the inside of the eye, and the
giant peony print of the walls like
a Rorschach blot of her DNA snarling …

Some of us are doing our homework,
and some of us have already done it, fast, in class,
and are up in our rooms pretending

to be about fractions and positions
of soldiers but the looming "*is*"
has got us in its maw
and we are reading to make for it a room.

Later there will be a diagnosis, that will be
to the complexity of the girl
with the hot tentacles of thought
tangled up in what someone in a book
has also thought, what
one word is to the hundred-fold-wood-smell
of the adult reading room at the library.

But *shhh,* now. We are with the girl.
Hating and thanking and minding
the book that mines our mind.

Tuscaloosa and Beyond

7 hrs 24 min 380 miles long 1mile wide Apr 27 EF4 tornado 3 syllables

Styrofoam chunk, the size and shape of SS *Bama Belle*.
Body chunks the student climbed over to call Mom.

Bayoneted pines puncturing pools of violet dark where
still-circling satellites spew pics of forest-sculpture,

open-fracture bridge, stroller-flags, whole-school corpse,
train in its new glass orchard festooned with tracks

while swirling pink insulation's
myriad toupees missing their bald heads

hunt something, *something,* somewhere, some
huge thing, some something, down.

And leaves, soaked, orphaned, exiled—oak, magnolia, book.
And sheaves of heat rebuilding

ghostly shapes of buildings over ideas of buildings and
reflector-dogs' snort and transformers' giddy swing and the urine

stench and the pump of the
mile-foot dredging panic up to

the manic stack that
tosses all the stuff and what the stuff is

made of and who owned or lived in it, up—

Hikmet, poet-Turk,
a prison-lifetime for his views,

calmed himself by conjuring "the things I didn't know I loved"—
a patient mile-high poem-dredge of sweet assembled junk—

and chronic Proust in chronic rooms
stockpiled, slow-spun, re-spun, years, but

time-sucked us can't meditate on how
what we know we loved here's, even if it's here, gone:

now we see straight through from Hargrove to 15ᵗʰ,
from have to have not, from ravishing to rending,

some just starting to take stock in ill-lit little hovels,
some taking water meat god blankets cigarettes some

sheared under shreds of girders throbbing to
sky's wild under-brain, O Roil and Tithe, what's

this peel-back to core of...?
O larger language O havoc-house O earth

Dream of the Cat on Three Legs

The fourth leg, closed up
like a wing against the body,
shudders, unhinging slightly with each step

which makes the animal look like it itself is dreaming
in wing-pumps, the chest muscle
twitching to get it to fly,

or else it's something else, something invisible
as breeze-teeth pulling
wing-meat apart at the joint—

but still the cat keeps coming toward you in its
jumbled lurch,
piqued cries peppering tender

inches as it gets closer, closer to you, *hew-mann*,
whose job, you've read,
whose job is to taste, dear god, and see

can you write this down yes I
can write this down the
wet glistening on the thickened paw the

re-opened crack exuding inky pus ...
What would it write, if it could,
the cat, or the ink?

Would it say how it came to be installed
by the workmen in the dream
here in its new station

on the pillow outside the screen door
to the Office of the Starving Particular
so that when they check in here, as they must,

the Makers of Art—in the dream, you are one of them,
one of the wearers of lavish headgear
fashioned for the jagged brain-peaks of the uselessly brave—

they must bear to be greeted by this host,
and must decide whether to go with
those on the left who pet it and quickly wash their hands,

or those on the right who step over it,
or those who never enter
this office,

taking, instead, the nail,
the nail and the snake bite inside them,
the hot tearing of flesh inside them,

the dagger of glass in the bone, inside,
cradling it,
nuzzling....

Your suffering weighs what it weighed
before you ever got here.
What happens here weighs what it weighs.

And *suffering* rhyming with *purring*—
a twin thing you wake with your mouth around—
also weighs what it weighs.

Palette

She has come a long dry way
zone upon zone

to awaken on the floor of the
friends of friends of friends

on the thin palette in the warehouse
curtained into something like rooms in

another of them close by
whoever-they-are making

a kind of machine of love
a soundtrack as she studies

a spidery map to his flat's
street address of ether she

told passport control best
she could where she was bound

then something in a bottle then stale
cartridges of bread the pleasantries

of the dispossessed
her new her certified kin

then a meager shower in the single hour
of hot water stolen off the grid

and donning of the packed
single gorgeous raiment

and looking up of digits and writing them on a slip
for when she phones herself in hell

no it's the number she keeps of a man
lately returned to Berlin

elite purveyor of flowers
in a cart across from the zoo

that fund his furious paintings God how she loved
the nineteen shades of blood and gouged-

out letter-like back-lit glyphs and
fucking in the tyrant's language

Gifts

D.D.

Books, your books, and blocks
of darkest chocolate on my desk,
luscious, vicious.

And the vintage paper doll kit,
"Instant people, for your first house!"—
conjoining wedding-cake skirts and stovepipe hats and cats
of the tribe of the continuous tail
and real nesting Russian dolls, her joke about the inner life,
where it gets women …

And, How to Make a Fire:
pre-soaked logs from the A&P,
little rocker drawn up so close the rockers smoke—

Incendiary queen.
Her subjects.

Thresh and Hold

It is not enough
        to hold onto your view.

Things in their ardor
        disregard a cause.

That the door is closed,
        is *that* door, is *there,* is

itself, is not other than it was.
        But mocks your highest time.

Months since she's written …
        moths since she's written …

enths that have shriven … moths
        eat a mitten …

you could
        take time and chop it

into a hundred skies and pin
        them to the wall

but—browns, blues—
        there is still nothing there.

A little
        red, maybe,

where the string around your old heart
　　　brushed a zone, and dried.

Some wind still
　　　frames the frames.

Vigil. Summer. Alabama.

A withering green that sags to yellow and yellow
that chokes on brown and brown collapsing to the color of everything.

Chipmunks, little fists of dust.
Hummingbirds broken in half.

Every morning the word *morning* stuck to the flowers' tongues.
Every evening time rubbing itself raw.

Who's been interrogating earth?
What did they do to make her crack?

The yard man showing up to shave
the scabs off the grass so he can eat.

Digits rising. More Alabama boys
enlisting in the sand.

In the field, every ear shriveled. The sun giving orders
to a convention of the deaf.

Where we are cut, a brief, sidereal rust.
What if not a drop appears in the upcoming history of earth?

Jay: a blue powder
sprinkled over the outlines of the lesser finches.

The magnolia doesn't even stink.
Eventually color won't exist.

We've taken to rising en masse,
embarking upon the still-dark hours

with quiet, similar voices.
Tired beasts. Slack leashes. Other tired beasts.

By noon, since lunch exists, outside the mission
crisp brown camos ignite in the wheelchairs' gleam.

Epistle to Unrelenting Days

To the sleek sides of missiles

      and rough intent

To air in its sickness

      of holy bent

To coming days

      if there be days

To dazzle and dredge

      mirage and the age

To turban of wind

      to presence of mind

To mercy and the many

      and to the far few

To whine and gasp

      simplistic and simplicity

To those among us

      who dwell not among us

To anger that augers

      to save us and, bless us,

To power collapsed upon

      power, collapsed

To sins of a father

        that blunder, blinder

To the brink

        to break bread

To shawl

        and shroud

To syllables shorn

        of veil and vile

To cries in that language

        to cry, in that language

To you who would singe

        to ye who go down singing

The List

D.D.

In the day's last light   eye-high   there
less than a hand's   reach into   the holly
the fledgling's stiff legs   chopsticks   jut up
out of the twig bowl where
how to say it
the red crested head was
ground to spice   the moment   of your vanishing
so loud   ringing the void   so complete   it
pulverized this   fragile antenna   so pungent
it swept on through all the world's creatures
divining   as your poems did   their course

Then all night long
a windy bush-shaped   sharp red song
scorching the dark   scolding

Who hung the homemade suet
that beckoned my enemies close?
This was my turf my zone my loves
my puffy tattered earthly home—
You helped? Now look what you've gone and done!

Oh bird-gone-into-the-dark
who sets my whole life-list aflame
at the mention of your public name

In My Thorn Dream

The thing is the delicacy
of the interwoven twig-vest
hovering, not quite touching,
but breathing a little when I breathe as
wreath and *wraith* prickle and twitch
inside in the organ
the dream drinks its milk from and

how out there in the forest but still inside the dream the
cyclone dips its eggbeater down and leaves
the shivering carpet of twigs: yes, that is the birth of it, the place the
woodsman, the woods-being, stands, weaving
ferocious vestments
while the twigs are still hot …

Outer, inner.
A thing, some Thing
I must do or
be sure not to.

I am standing very still
in my vest of thorns.
I don't think you can touch me yet.
But, someone with salve, now.
But, someone with bandages.
Whether I too will be needed …

I seemed, until *this,* to be on my way—

II

The Old Feeder

In our old life the treehouse sufficed
as a place to hang it,
being grand and of an angle
like the prow of a ship
out over the manicured lawn.
In our old life the birds were pets,
and asked to be counted
and we counted them.

And when the child said
It's-an-eagle! we said
Why-not-an-eagle! though eagles
were not on the check-off life-list
in the bird book of that particular state.

And when the child said
red-headed for *red-bellied*
we marked it off anyway, one
specialness being as worthy as another
and whoever named the birds
none the wiser.

And it all sufficed for a time.
When asked about pets he said
tufted titmouse, and when asked
his favorite sport he said
over-and-back, over-and-back
for how they hack seeds open one-
at-a-time between their boots,

and so it seemed life adopted us,
or we adopted life,
or it adapted, or we
meant to.

And when the bully woodpecker shattered
half-a-tube to smithereens
we enriched the mix to bring out
his better nature, though this
short-lived kindness
was of the glancing kind.

And once we bought a month's feed
and paid a neighbor kid
to husband our odd troops while we
took a trip to an aged country,
the ground a mess of shit and shells
when we returned.

And over years the bin lid yawned
and rats got in the seed
and rain rained in
and webby fingers grew

and the boy outgrew nature
in a way that broke my heart
or was it that we'd somehow
all this time failed to feed him

and water got scarce
our chattering turned rancid
lightning guillotined
tree and treehouse back to lumber

and where the birds went, then,
and whether or what they ate
I never knew, being so divorced
from song itself, nor what
the boy petted nor what
the hollow bones filled with
nor who belied whose markings till

the thing lay in a box,
inner seed tube cracked,
its foothold-cage a clueless crossword

words

cross with me,
surrendered as I had
to drought, reigning dust,
a shatter shattering the sky—

around my eyes
the dinosaur-lings'
anisodactyl claws
stamped, stamped, their sharp, 3-pronged
stars, stars, stars,

and I let out the squawk my
dry-human-cry—

so. I take it from the box.
Stab it on its pole.
And measure off the distance
to the squirrel-free center of this
hard yard, calling something—*winged,* please—
down into the center of this my clearing my fledgling my life.

Early Riser

You go along in a darkness
—years, leagues—
you go along in a darkness,
the light at the world's edge
falling off your eye
again

You go along in the darkness
of the inside of the body
filling in the eye craters flowing
into sleep your sleep
cementing up the space
between needing and getting, and pawing

through your dream where
the gunmetal
taste of blood
is how the flowers smell
on the rare occasions
the dream-flowers dare flower

You keep going on in a darkness
that spans a rickety bridge
and many barrel staves

Now that you are older it's
become a witnessing darkness
the way
time tilts
away from the light
just *is*

and the tragedies of others are
a paint time has been dipped in
by a hand, except the hand
was never there

Now a count is taken in the dream
of how many units of darkness get
ladled over your head vs. the next head
and some figure raises the question
of who gets how much darkness
and whose eyes are staked forward watching
another, darkening,
then in the next frame
a figure figures it up on a chart:

Two oily depths for you, Dearie, and three silent
implosions for you to witness, My Little Quince,
and for you, My Blurry One, who both *is* and *sees* in ink,
four boatloads of the meds
that tint the darkness a color from The Book of Colors
called "pale fawn cut down to its knees"
while the darkness keeps getting darker
on the Great Tongue that licks the graph clean

And when you demand more answers to this question
of the fairness of the meting out of the darkness
the question whinnies and sways
and plunges back down
to the poet's dark hair on the ground
filling with particular blood
the mother's nerves' husks stripped off

the child crying his dark purple cry
hour upon stuttering, heaving hour
the flute drying to a stick in its case
the elders objecting to the species of weed
rising out of their ashes
hope itself scant saffron

So that when he returns in the morning,
back to you in the morning
to you still in this dream
in the stock-still, faintly-spiced, still-darkened room,

back from his golden coffee,
back from his matin salutations
and davenings to the void,
back from his and his fellow creature's
six-legged fig tree and blueberry inspections,
back with the present of the present,

when this early riser comes back
rinsed in the light of day
to pull you up and hold you
accountable to light
this other, this speechless stunned dream-clad she
this dizzy inky girl
rises alongside you
and he takes you—he knows this—
takes both of you up in his arms.

It is not always possible to fall in love in blackberry season

You might enter the many dark chambers
 without this tender clustering,

you might start by washing your lover's mouth in snow
or tease apart the spring tendril root of him,

or scrape the old leaves out of his autumn hair
on your way to making his acquaintance in loam,

but if it is chosen in the kingdom of blackberries
that you shall be one of the ones,

one of the many clusters of ones,
that among the thorns and giant snails

you and he shall wade the slimy,
primordial rocks of the creek

to get to the blackberries leaning over the current,
and if whoever sees one first

shall place it onto the waiting, snail-like
ravenous tongue of the other

and know the gift of
the other's pleasure before he

dismantles with his gentlest caliper fingers
the next dark ripe one, leaving

the brightness for later,
the suck and give

of the pale, moist, naked, astonished stem-head
among the young screaming red ones for later

and place that next, that dark, that ripe one on your tongue
so that always, when you kiss, the explosion

of ankle-breaking cold and warm purple liquid earth
will alarm and comfort you

back to the beginning
of gathering everything in sight,

the ruin already in it, the bleeding
and the rot and plundering birds already in it,

a sharp, riotous darken-ness already in it, then

will you be ready
to lay your lives, together, down in thorns?

Bus Stop Reel

-times, whilst waiting for the bus, my feet start to move and it is not even at all a little bit in the least ever so slightly subtle. Feet start-to start-to move. Better set-my shop-ping down-cause. Feet start-to start-to move. Get-ting real-em bar-rass ing-but. Feets. Start-to start-to go. Back to their true origins. In mist. Or as rough hooves or claws. What coup or kick they're plotting …

Some. Times you dream of me. Raw daylight I'm. Ascending gritty. Stairs. To the bus whilst. Thinking of your quadriceps. And you. Knowing what I do. Or do. Not wear beneath. My skirt. Which you won't ever know unless the bus material-

izes. Which. Hasn't happened. Yet it's gotten. Wolfishly cold. Here is. An icicle to pen this tune in wolf-peed snow. Art has. High purposes like warming the inside of the. Brain with its. Intricate rhythmical. Fires. Which are

always near. By. Like in *The. Inheritors* a. Favorite book. Of my dead dad's. He. Liked the image of. The peat ball always carried. By the. Puniest ape-kid he. Related to. The infinite smouldering and the sense. It wasn't just. About individual hanker-

ing. He. Would have liked you for your. Eager etymologies. And how you waltz with me. And how you make your mouth a. Soft nest when you say my name. Even if it wasn't a bird's. Though the fact it iz. A bird's and a man's. Iz extra lovely. Some-

times, whilst waiting for the bus my feet they start to move. Better set my shopping down it's getting real em. Barrassing. Back to their true origins. In mist or as rough hooves or claws. This will keep on looping till the bus de. Cides to come. Some-

Bus Stop Reel

by Anita Anderson

Treeline

Those treeline pines
horizon to horizon
writing one long cursive word?

Stay in me till you've said it.

The Shining

for my mother

It is the beginning of her shining
and the beginning of her shining hour.
She has had the dream about the woman in white
and entered her shining final hours.

It is the essence of her leaving,
the leavening of what has been borne.
A white tear off the edge of her voice,
walking toward her, full blown.

The woman, coming over a hill.
A shining woman cresting the shining hill,

trailing my mother's name from her mouth
like a scarf of white bees,
lacey-white-clover-honey
death-words in her mouth.

It is where I am not meant to be.
This daughter, not meant to be.
I am certainly not the woman in white
and neither, yet, is she.

I am not the nurse she tells it to
and I am not the gown made of liquid light
and I'm still not the one who ought to tell this tale
lest she hear me from her side of the hill.

It was her own mother, with plenty of time.
It was a creature of recompense and sense
and it was her Snowball, the white cat, found.

And it was like when she fished or cooked,
getting it right, giving patience its form.
It was a snow-choked Zhivago final scene
and her own painting painting her own white hand.

(It was not her previous version,
the white-clad night nurse shaking her loose
as a limp-headed doll, and this time nothing
was noted in the chart since there was nothing
to dutifully follow-up on and deduce.)

How do the dead come for the dead?
What is our job and what will it be?
What happens in the crossing that the face is lost?
By whom, by what feature, shall our promises be bound?

It was two days before, and meant to be.
Prelude of her crossing to receive herself,
the self's most pretty self saying *yes* and *come with me,*
so, when my sister finished singing her across,

my sister singing, singing her across,
singing every hymn and Irish ballad she knew,
the only one there was the white one who heard
the shining in that singing, and so my mother flew.

Still Life with Box Turtle and a Box of Chocolates

You can tell she's a *she*
from the brown eyes

it's like an abstract turtle-claw shape
has walked all over her own back

golden claw gestures haloing
palm-shaped shapes

like sugar dust marks
on the mound of expensive chocolates the chocolates

somehow
stamped there themselves

beauty has its ways
of obsessing

for instance loving you nearly
all morning

then taking my solitary walk and
—full monty of merit badges!—

ahem (but she cannot cough)
there she was in the road

loving you for instance at night
then there she was again, queen of our dream

what's beautiful is how beauty
goes on

claw, palm down
claw, palm up

flipping the oar in the oarlock
of turtledom

resting, then rowing
resting, then rowing

waiting a long time
to meet you

she can close completely
we know how that can be

and how parts of the self
can disappear

she can store sperm
for years   well

it was getting on toward
a hundred turtle years

carapace, blood, and nerve,
I'm finally yours

My Hair

When I gather my long
leaf-colored hair
and make of it a stem

and twist the handle of my head
and join it back to me
with metal pins

I'm on your lap again
my hands are in the air
my view is mile upon mile

I feel you fashioning the serpent
on my head and the thick braid
of you inside me

I'm ready now to enter
a prim public place
where I am the teacher the police a saint

I turn my back
and everyone I command
sees what it can be to be commanded

–O-O–

That dream of the glasses
that smear out everything
except what we hold near and dear?
These commodious wireframed O's
might just accommodate our budget and our needs!

And, handsome afterthought, Jerome
here at Target is great at fitting them,
beckoning from the other side
after we check out.
So good is Jerome, his framed certificates attest,
he belongs in a palace finessing crossbow sights,
eyeliner-ing eyes on the tails of lined-up peacocks,
but, no, he's customer-less, sleek, keen, seen:

a boy-god's is *his* frame—

and certain ones (pentagons?) are 75% off today, so
here we go …

for Jerome *is* progressive on our behalf—
has us gaze from close to distant target and back.
It will cost a bit more to go poetry-world-poetry
or is it world-poetry-world, though he
suggests for all-around living it's the way.

His own face is naked, 30-ish.
One wonders what he wonders but he seems
mightily trained, he should have
his own shop on the Promenade of Owls
where we could focus on feathers' grain, count distant mice,

but we seem to have decided and
he's scurrying, measuring, but what *did* we decide?

Did we go in for the distant-darkness special?
With full-ghost coating?
Assurance we won't be trashed
by normal wear and tear?

We're cozy with Jerome by now.
The lover who said we had such
gorgeous wide-set eyes was not in the ballpark of what Jerome
notes with his handheld inverse muse machine that gazes
down our gaze and makes us his tender subject.

Oh dry-palmed prince, who loves not the eagle-eyed young
but, rather, stylish *us* so rapt upon the diadem of flesh
twixt his eyes, we confess the rest:

There is, of late, Jerome, of late, a murk, that lurks—
images carousing from one scene to the next,
hawkish clouds washing over the book of deserts,
desserts without borders and a clotting
of seagulls every time we comb our hair—

We are, we say, *detaching,* but not from
our tipsy loved ones and certainly
not from you who comprehends the uber-
importance of this work and is working up
our picks—prisms, inches, tint, tilt— but there are, Jerome,

two worlds, two worlds
that, we see now, seem always to have been ...

When we wash our four hands there's
the the faucet faucet and
twin towers of water and the
drain draining the drain ...

J.J., which of us *is?*
Is our sight in your sights?
Is you fixing our fix?

Well, he says, there are, he says, others
we *could* go to, a kind of work we still just
might have time to do
if they'd take us, and enroll us
among the pirate patches, child-sized chairs and cheery coaches
(picture us, our privacies and churlish airs and leery voices).
But for now, let's see ...

We do! We really do!
At least enough to drive us home.
Or someone does. That's what *they* do.

Please Don't Sell the 308

For the Brylcreem smell is from my flying dream.

For there are no cup holders so we must drink the air.

For the wipers are shredded buffalo hide and the roll bar doesn't exist.

For it was forged long ago in the furnace where the top was pried off the earth.

For my hair, flying, and your hair, flying, make a twisted rope the air can climb.

For the passenger door handle is frozen like grim fate but my right hip flexor leaps gazelle-like over the edge.

For the 5K we'd get for it would fix my tooth so well it would be all that's left of me in the afterlife but I'd rather go toothless into the wind.

For our ineptitude deserves a parade lap.

For the road begged me to beg you.

For my flying dream gets better mileage than your flying dream.

For the dogs nap in it.

For the surgeon you bought it from drove the blood off his hands in it.

For the interior is buttery maroon.

For it has a back seat anyone's past life can stretch out in.

For the recent ice age provides the A/C.

For the tape deck whirs and flips and bows to the thieves of music.

For I know a secret garage that matches your secret garage.

For the clutch is the clutch of ruination but you are my antennae's little flag.

For the original inhabitants are toast but their shell remains, a glittering tomb.

For the gas tank's aswirl with glittering bone flecks

of the dinosaur revving up his big-boy dream.

Quarry Cross

My head on your shoulder,
my leg thrown over,
your hand in my hair,
your other hand, there.

My sigh like the lessening light
going finally, all the way, out to sea,
my combs on the table like lashes able
to see what deep quarry creatures see.

Red Rover, Red Rover, and then you roll over,
your knees drawn up in the dark.
Old stars above you, old stars below you,
old starlight blanketing the ground,

you lean out over your old wooden skis
and go ahead again. You let yourself fall.
And turn up the slope. And fall. And turn.
And dare that sweet abyss.

My mouth on your ear,
my shadow worn sheer.
Your dust in my voice,
this kingdom of choice.

Red Rover, Red Rover, now let me turn over
my memory knotted with sticks from the day
we hiked the hills that rose like hopes
of something, something, trying to pray

toward the quarry signposted that-a-way—
behind me your steady footfall-voice,
a cough, sting, blood, my backward glance
but the quarry entrance was not erased.

Red Rock, Red Thunder, then we, together,
gazed over the ragged rim:
a blood-rust, bone-worn planet-gash,
a man-plundered, bombed-out, gap-gawked space

and did what we could to make amends
—crumbs for the crows
—an altar of stones
meagerest meaning, tiny recompense,

then skidded like tears down its skeleton face
to lay in that missing meteor's bed
and seek the smooth skull of each other's head
and kiss the ancient dust away,

myself thrown wide to the beam of you
we made a moment's quarry cross.
A human flickering, at most.
A flickering quarry cross.

The Quarry Cross

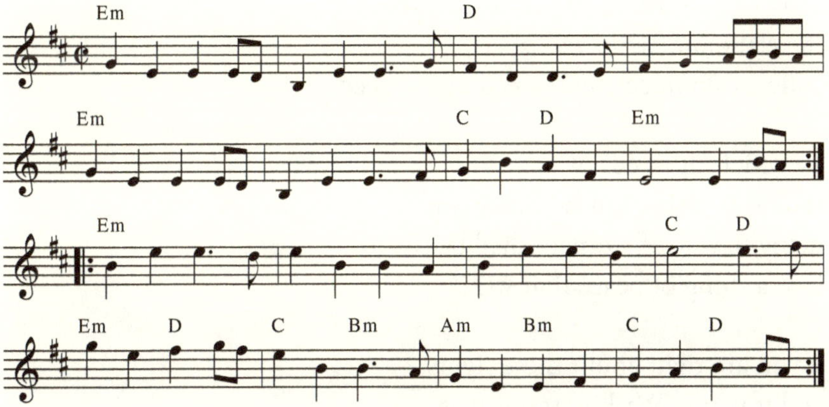

The Rights of Man

Here you are again, Tom Paine,
constructing from scratch like a cake
the elaborate organized layers,
concept upon concept, creed upon creed,

by which the seeds of man,
the many rising kinds of men and
many flavors of women, shall be shaped
into a thing of peace that will,

if you are right about these rights,
and if young Washington listens,
be a ceaseless Rube Goldberg contraption of a jolly good self-
perpetuating country the way God on Their best
good-hair day dreams.

Molecular? Spectacular? Oracular? Vernacular?
What shall this song be, your music that calls
from the gizzard of the common man
a listing of his rights, his left-behinds, his thefts,
his faintest inclinations toward the good that,
rightly codified, could shine?

We have some rights today.
We're mostly fed, and mostly said
to be allowed to vote, love, dance, and
marry whom we please,
safely get sick if the boss has a plan,
and vote and piss at will if we are not in jail.

On rights, you were right, Tom Paine.
We've kept the *e* that ends your name.
We wouldn't want it said again
how, given rope, we'd, ourselves, hang
on to what you said. Dear Tom.

Dear. Beautiful. Dead. "Thoughtful optimist" man.
We want the stuff you knew about. The stuff
that isn't stuff. We want the system wherein
we are kingless, queenless, none of that fluff.
We want for God to tell us to put down
our cardboard burger crowns, dear peoples,
on the sacred ground.
Down come the crowns! Mums' crowns, dads' crowns,
thee and me crowns. A million zillion heads of state
all equal, on the ground. It's a dance we do,
or listen to. We want our rights. We won them. They're

the right to pose as our true selves.
The right to drink ourselves to death.
The right to ink the tattoo down into our starving heart
and change our mind again.
Tom Paine, thanks for *The Rights of Man*.
Your rights were right. We've set them so. We even have a song that goes:

The Rights of Man

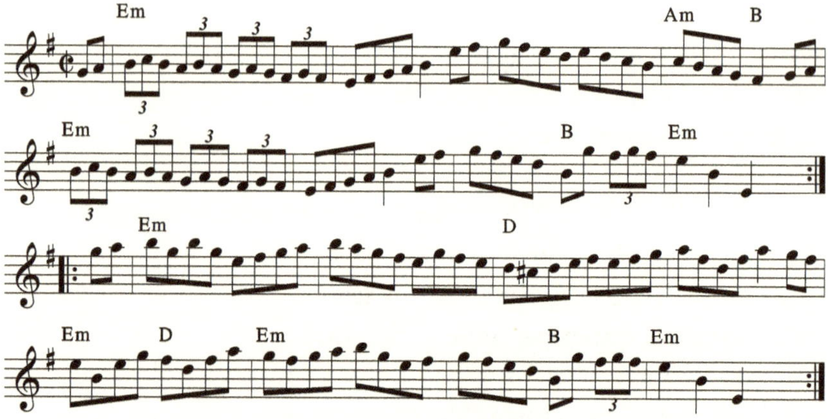

Elegy and Lament

for my mother

Sometimes words flock down
      phlox, elder
the whole air a nest,
      older, alder
a thicket of tones
      attune, atone

in my hair or underneath me
      fox, recur
or at my side where a dog would be
      leash, plush
or a calm child if such a
      mew, mewl

calm child exists, and somehow I am saved
      comet, helmet
a little bit saved
      egret, regret
from her silence pouring through me
      moon, strewn

ever since the thing I did
      galaxy? manatee?
since some thing I must have done
      rubber, raincoat, publish, polish,
      under, under, plunder, her
made the whole air red
      stitch, graze, slice, stain

I'm saved, too, from how she died
    hospice, trespass
hating the nurses
    pale, impale
claiming they were shaking her
    Megan, vegan
in the middle of the night
    lullaby, alibi

and from how certain words
    tray, button, clipboard, purse
forsook her in the end
    thank, you
actually months and years
    please, dear
before the end
    love you

Orphan words, do you come from
    offering, suffering
where she went
    stalwart, homeward
or from an inner-ether
    soul-slough, cell-glow

or from the membrane in my dream
    latex, pretext
she pressed her teeth against
    hollow, allow
or from wherever art
    tombs tombs

waits to be made
  glad, glade

She liked to take a walk
  Wallabee, wannabe
but wouldn't say why
  hide, cry
and she liked her tea
  steep, green
so full of adjectives
  ginger, laced, iced, peach, dragonfly-tinged
it hadn't room left
  highball, snowball
for being merely liquid
  nectar, succor

If life could have been all
  pearly, impervious
customized essences
  straight A, bug spray

she would have faired better
  terminator, aviator
Maybe that comes free
  ether, mother
where she is now
  there, now

Here the tall wildflowers
    girls, boys
meet pink horizontal breeze
    marvel, scarves
a little too high up
    atmosphere, stratosphere
to render a nod
    prod, proud

Why couldn't it end like this
    crossword, clueless
at the coordinates of yes
    detain, détente
a laying-down of harms,
    Maggie, gimme
her essence in my arms
    worn, warm

The Old Harms

Here are the old harms in a pot. Of course we must call it a cauldron. A cauldron of old harms. And because we have made that correction, we must be one of the ancient ones—crones, ogres, toppled queens— we feel our outlines torn from the ragged pages of a book, our button eyes of ink still drying as we look through them.

What shall we do with the old harms that keep us in our shredded cloaks, long-handled spoons in our spindle hands? We would like to be done with this and return to the fluorescence of the modern, but first we must dispense with the old harms. If we spread them on the landscape like a mist or a paint, they will get on our sight and stay there, so we are still with the giant cauldron—they don't make cauldrons like this these days so we know this stirring we have been doing is as old as dirt, as the harms.

Is there a fire under the pot? There might not even be a fire anymore. Is there a steam rising from the pot that can be smelled across the land? Not even a steam. What if we stop stirring, then? What if we throw the spoons in and let the universal solvent of old harms dissolve the wooden spoons and paddles right down into the mess, some extra fiber in the soup, what then? No one was willing to eat this mux anyway. No one was coming to the meal though we sent out so many invitations all across the land and on our best ponies at that. Not a soul except the souls here conjured, fairly or unfairly, by these old harms, up. Maybe our life will be spent here, teetering at the black lip of the cauldron, and maybe we will put a little cauldron-kohl under our eyes for that penetrating come-here-baby-so-I-can-harm-you-equal-to-the-ballast-of-my-own-harms effect, or maybe we will blink twice and find ourselves in a clearing with gobs of green shoots sprung up from cauldron-colored earth, or maybe we will look down and see little carrot greens and delicately excise them and make a soup, and the vitamin A will do wonders for our vision such that we will no longer misperceive the pointed faces of old harms.

And it seems to be a permanent job, 24/7/52/365, this bending over tending to the pot. Which would explain the stoop of the ages and the aged.

We try walking away from the pot but the pot gets up and follows us on its chicken-bone legs. What we decide to make of it is an artistic movement in which each chicken-legged pot-bellied pot is paraded on a rhinestone leash. And it an artistic encompassing "ism"— potism, despotism, nepotism, dismalism, chickenism—the legs peck out a manifesto in the dirt the wind all but erases, but the stain of the thing still stays. A charred place deep in a forest. What might have been said to her to save her. And how, forevermore, she refuses to say anything back.

The Needs

Anyway, the needs. The many needy needs
here at the Conference of Needs where we are
revving up the day with our dead mom's favorite coffee cup
we wrapped, Gumby handle-arm glued
back to its hip, packed, unpacked, and filled up
from the conference carafe.
Next resident of earth in line's pawful
of pills is downed with Joe, then
the next one circles, banking around the bagels
and the next, an old soul whose
Tinwoodsman armor shines, has coalesced, already
having eaten or not planning to, hovering like a rare vaccine
next to the one with the phone above her heart.
Then, last in line at the buffet, hearing aids
snuggled in her pocket like snails under a leaf,
the one who seems to star in every single story in the Times
the way she's searching for a face or fact, the paper in front
of her a verbose gravestone, hers.

Brochure: "The Gathering."
Dance Only and Couples rates.
We might be able to afford soap, foxtrot.
As we were saying, Needs. We mostly
stumble on with them on leashes getting petted or
our heart is dog meat and they chew themselves
or pump themselves up, or they are met—petting
behind the ears, on underbellies, heart—
commencing at the proper time and constantly since then.

We go on through our seven days.
Lapels, deep V-necks, swanky specs.

In between the nametags and the coffee and MetLife,
breakout options:
    1. Clouded Money
    2. World Piece
    3. Planet Gardening since
    4. Monster Floods have softened us and dirt and
    5. Island Outlines
Lunch already! Sandwiches! slathered with air, or not,
in the grand ballroom of the afternoon.

Brochure: "Innumerables." Rounds, peps, slides.
No head counts, so no way to know who's in whose room
though dancing's soon. The old soul's
still out posing by the human-made lake, working on
the "Statue of Today" she has been working on.
Pills' half lives live on.
Wheat heat safely undulates the distant picturesque.

Mom would have liked these
smart people in this paintable place and flirted with
the profs. You could be her but it's been done.
Your need limps on. Why have you come. You miss
the keynote nap, fast-forward to C major hopes, a thimbleful of
        liquids, notes,
a little practice time. Everything's a band name
bandnamegenerator.com says is taken and suggests instead
"Riders of the Gaelic Gray" for $25.
Your band, you think, would not have disbanded
with a name like that. You snap your wristband,
a pain you know is good like the spine-curdling bell
at the Hall of Koans Camp you went to last year.

Maybe you'll go back there, where the topics are The Air is Air and
Here is Here, but never Needs are Needs.
Need.com's conglomerate could take over all camps.

But first there's supper
by the lake so all the dogs can come.
You lost your dog. It jumped, and died.
Who knew dog life was hard?
Your friend's needs, writ large, seemed met,
what with the succulence she kept digging up.
She'd gone all-state flute once, but then
all-statue like the angel on her double-grave
already there, voilà.

But you've constructed, in a breakout,
wheels, a sort of skateboard-with-a-rope
her whole need would have fit on (once, in a restaurant,
you saw four women wheel their fifth friend's torso tenderly in—
belly-down, she chewed …) and yours too.
To pull it sort of suits you, meets your need, this day.
Since everything's been paid.

Blue October

By the time the angel thinks to enter the scene
half of the theater is gone—

no not half of the audience half
of *place* itself, sheared away.

She comes from behind a lopped column
topped with a valence of blood

that leaks from another theater above
in which your seat has been assigned

so you can watch her wind her
way down

and make a muffled entrance
in the required leaf-shaped shoes.

She leaves no particular trace.
Her prints are what

a child would make
with a carved potato stamp.

She paces before the flickering
apertures of the moments of her life

she could visit again,
trying to decide which one.

Everywhere, piles of leaves
and the burnt smell of misgiving.

Once she takes off her shoes there will be only
the single yellow feather

she will carry like a lamp
into the inner chamber

and lay down with a little flourish
like a gentleman's cape across a puddle

to protect his love's new shoes—
at the threshold of the inner-inner

chamber where three guards stand tall as sticks.
From above—if "above" and "you" exist—

the choir does another smoky song
about life or death or the changing of the seasons.

Whoever can pass by this scene intact
will either swim forever

in blue October
where nothing and no one ever finishes falling

or drift like a spark up to the underside of heaven
and add a hundred years to the fire.

And her?
She's gone. It's done.

The Hummingbird Feeder

It takes a telepathic cajoling
and much sterilizing
and dastardly ant outsmarting
and a relinquishment of the possibility of ever, really, controlling
anything and the courage to sense that you, yourself, are also very small

on earth, and a bit of cooking—
oh, you, whose calves are slashed, working
in the cane fields, starving
on the price of sugar, bringing in
the harvest to feed the human need for sweetening,
forgive our measuring
the dutiful four-to-one, boiling
water-to-bonafide-cane, owing
to the fact that anything
other, wild honey, untame aspartame, could, notwithstanding
pure intentions, kill.

It takes, additionally, hanging
tough in the face(s) of grunting
foes: bee snorting past, jay laughing
his cruel blue laugh, column of squirrels running
flat out, ladder across their backs, pinning
the landing, flying, needle-straw jutting
out from the first one's squirrely lips, that crippling
idea, that others must be wanting what we want, flying
through the skull—.

Hollyhocks, forgive our wanting
the gift you already have of providing
actual succor. The type that's so essential it's leaning

toward world peace, and you don't even care about having
it. But I have a yin for pulsing.
For the little sleeve of muscle, the quivering
green thumb-cigar lit at the throat, blurring
then not. Those gazillion heartbeats resting
on the red plastic petal-stamped rim
where I might see its secrets, and, if it is grinning
and the grin is very young, inside the mouth a shining
surprise: yellow! so your mom, or us, can see and, being
bound, do our best to respond, heading off the suffering
that makes some grown-ups shrill, or chill, or dull.

See what you do to time?
How centuries of wretchedness and human bleeding
come down to this *now* (Audubon's guns retreating),
this window-watching woman pleading:
Alight! Be of the earth! Just be! And be filled.

In My Path Dream

Cinqua Terra

Hello, lofty selves, still gliding
velvet feet along this outcrop's famous footpath
the landslide had its way with!

And hi!, Swiss Spiderman-ish engineers and mountaineers!
Your chain-link doilies, pinioned, keeping overhead overhead,
your lonely mutant soccer net daring boulders to bowl,
your helicoptered tonnage of bags of dry cement and hulking,
       wobbly water blocks,
your cantilevered Band-Aids that straddle, once again,
the picturesque abyss!

Your toils mean we got to snap
some memorable brain pictures
so now, in sleep, we sweat again, still dreamily traversing
from one pastel sun-blanched villa-toffee-clump wedged into a cliff
to the next pastel sun-blanched villa-toffee-clump wedged into the
      next cliff
all daggering down to the sea—

Behind us, mid-trek, -mirage,
the town we slept etc. in.
Ahead's the next one up the coast where
—as it was foretold in the book—lunch exists!

It's our turn for life!
Our go at ankle-torque!
At asthma and miasma of

ancient trail of head-size rocks
whose eerie faces have the smooth

complexion of a face transplant from some sun-beaten
comrade who laid them one by heavy one,
a lifetime to advance the cause some feet toward the
next hamlet so his great, no, his great-great, no, his
mega-great granddaughter might,
by path, come across a slightly strange-looking lad
with vibrantly variant genes,

the thing about keeping on *being* being the thing
less traveled by, but still, in dream/life, traveled *toward,* by
her, him, them, us…

that, and how we hold those
lovers/builders/fixers in our minds,
which, in the dream, we *know* about—
both our minds and the minds they hold—
Are they in your mermaid purse?—

like dried black skate eggs' cases
touching thready arms
at their own brittle peril in a jar
we have carried all this way because it might be,
it might, it might represent—*Are they? Are they?* —
we might let it be for us one fragile, hopeful—*Are they?*—mind
we take turns with from shoulders to shoulders
like the backpack,
like big gear,
like the idea itself of the idea itself…

The things we have done and will do
on either end of the kingdom of our dream
are very busy being clouds that mount, that fall apart.
Cliffward, toy trains could spirit us away.
Seaward, the toy boats that beat us to our town
know all ye need to know,
writing constant arrowheads on waves.

Mairi's Wedding

Step we gaily, on we go
Heel for heel and toe for toe
Arm and arm and row and row
All for Mairi's wedding

Over hillways up and down
Myrtle green and bracken brown
Pass the shilling through the town
All for the sake of Mairi

The part I woke up singing was the chorus, the jaunty heft, Mairi from behind, her long hair not flowing as much as writing on the air for it was an air and I was playing in a band, a band of villagers and a rubber band and a band with an *and* and a pick-up band, I was playing my wooden flute, the one I'll get in 3000 when my number comes up in deepest Asheville, a town made all of ashes of the druid tree they torched to extract the one pure flute they make replicas of now.

I was next to the mandolin and you were playing your fiddle hung around your neck by a contraption of ribbons and gleaming birds and spaghetti though they don't make spaghetti in the country where Mairi lives, where she survives to this day on unpasteurized hummingbird milk. It was a folk thing. I thought to myself, if I were Mairi it would be cool to be folksy, unashamed of loving eight bar phrases where the tonic always comes round again as all the dancers' feet come down like a herd of elks stepping up to the bar at the same time where the tonic is in the glasses designed for elk lips and they all sip at once, going forward and back, or, alternatively, like hairy lassos on fire. Arm and arm and heel and toe, a twister game, Mairi in junior high, her first smooch with that boy she will marry, the thing they'll make the song about, though if you told her that then she would have been grossed out and become a cheerleader instead of a milkmaid on the spot.

Everyone should have a song about themselves. Everyone should have someone write a song or a poem about them and that goes double for the ones gushing pixels at everyone else. So today Mairi's wedding is about our wedding notwithstanding it might be a challenge to pull off what with a fiddle for a stiff curvaceous tie and me in my mandatory naked dream attire. We will have to get dressed sometime or other in this life or decide to be clothed forever and always only in music. Meanwhile, there is much music we can play, especially old Irish tunes that reek of sweet milk, a little caveman nipple in them, a few floating hands-across-the-water we are not ashamed to hoist in a bobbing circle while we sing—even when, as occasionally happens in these dour flagrant days, there is something truly deeply lavishly happy to sing about.

Mairi's Wedding

Three Horses

Henceforth, three horses.
Dust- or rain-bedazzled.
Hot days or cool, days of wind
or merciful stillness, three, now, here,

three horses you must take
as long to look at as it took them
to become this triangle you could balance
a camera or lifetime or your suffering upon,

never just one horse anymore,
and never two woefully parallel horses,
but three, now, yes, three horses.
One called My Body and one called Your Body
and one called My Hooves in Your Hair.

NOTES

The poems accompanied by musical scores (noted below with an asterisk), are named after fiddle tunes—traditional jigs, reels, and a hornpipe—and are inspired by their titles, rhythms, and sounds. You can hear these tunes with the poems read inside them at robinbehn.com.

"irishtune.info" is a found poem.

*"The Cliffs of Moher": The Cliffs of Moher, Ireland's most visited natural attraction, rise 702 feet from the sea at their highest point on the southwestern edge of the Burren region in County Clare.

*"The Star above the Garter": "The Star above the Garter" may be a reference to the phrase "stars and garters," to numerous pubs named Star and Garter, or to The Order of the Garter whose emblem is a star.

"*I Never Promised You a Rose Garden*" refers to the novel by Joanne Greenberg.

"Thresh and Hold" is inspired by Mirjana Ugrinov's painting.

*"Bus Stop Reel"

*"Quarry Cross": The name of the tune refers to a crossroads at a quarry, or a road or path leading to a quarry.

*"The Rights of Man": *The Rights of Man* (1791) is a book by Thomas Paine as well as the name of this tune.

"Blue October" is inspired by Mirjana Ugrinov's painting.

*"Mairi's Wedding"

Acknowledgments

Grateful acknowledgment is made to these publications in which poems first appeared, sometimes in different versions:

The American Journal of Poetry: "Palette"

The Cape Rock: "Blue October," "The Old Feeder," "The Stanzas Combine at Dusk"

Crab Orchard Review: "Epistle to Unrelenting Days"

Crazyhorse: "Tuscaloosa and Beyond"

Eleven Eleven: "Dream of the Cat on Three Legs"

The Kenyon Review: "Shatter"

The Offending Adam: "Vigil. Summer. Alabama."

Plume: "I Never Promised You a Rose Garden," "The List," "Gifts," "Here at the Scene," "In My Thom Dream," "In My Path Dream"

Poetry: "My Hair"

A Poetry Congeries: "The Guild" as "The Writers' Guild"

Poetry London: "Inventory at Dusk"

The Superstition Review: "The Star above the Garter"

TAB: The Journal of Poetry and Poetics: "It is not always possible to fall in love in blackberry season," "The Shining"

Upstreet: "Elegy and Lament"

The Plume Anthology of Poetry 2013: "In a Vodka Vein," "Please Don't Sell the 308"

The Plume Anthology of Poetry 5: "The Needs"

The Plume Anthology of Poetry 6: "The Hummingbird Feeder"

Someone Else's Love Story, a novel by Joshilyn Jackson: a character writes "It is not always possible to fall in love in blackberry season."

Still Life with Poem: "Still Life with Box Turtle and a Box of Chocolates"

When She Named Fire: An Anthology of Contemporary Poetry by American Women: "My Hair"

"Bus Stop Reel" is used by permission of composer Anita Anderson. All other tunes are traditional.

The settings for all music notation were provided by Susan Songer. "Bus Stop Reel," "The Cliffs of Moher," "The Quarry Cross," and "The Star above the Garter" are included in *The Portland Collection: Contra Dance Music in the Pacific Northwest,* rev. ed., copyright © Susan Songer with Clyde Curley.

Many thanks to the Hambidge Center and The Ragdale Foundation for time and space. Thanks to Anita Anderson for "Bus Stop Reel" and to Susan Songer who went above and beyond to make all the music notation available. To Waxwing Band—"Traditional music taking flight!"—thanks for grand times playing memorable tunes. And to Danny Lawless and Marc Vincenz, editors non pareil, abiding gratitude.

ABOUT THE AUTHOR

ROBIN BEHN is the author of four previous volumes of poems including *The Yellow House* and *Horizon Note,* and two chapbooks. Co-editor of *The Practice of Poetry: Writing Exercises from Poets Who Teach,* and editor of a collection for young writers, *Once Upon a Time in the Twenty-First Century: Unexpected Exercises in Creative Writing,* she is a recipient of grants from the Guggenheim Foundation and the National Endowment for the Arts. Behn is also a musician, and has played flute and penny whistle with Waxwing Band and written the libretto for an opera, *Freedom and Fire! A Civil War Story.* Behn teaches in the MFA Program in Creative Writing at The University of Alabama and lives in Birmingham.